YOUR KNOWLEDGE HAS VALUE

Bibliographic information published by the German National Library:

The German National Library lists this publication in the National Bibliography; detailed bibliographic data are available on the Internet at http://dnb.dnb.de .

Imprint:

Copyright © 2014 GRIN Verlag
Print and binding: Books on Demand GmbH, Norderstedt Germany
ISBN: 9783656638803

This book at GRIN:

https://www.grin.com/document/271673

Paul Onwurah, Hyellamanda Musa, Tombari Biranen, Chidinma Orji, Don-mike Uwagwu, Abdul-Samad Mohammed

Women's participation in IT and technology. Reasons and solutions for the low participation

GRIN Verlag

GRIN - Your knowledge has value

Since its foundation in 1998, GRIN has specialized in publishing academic texts by students, college teachers and other academics as e-book and printed book. The website www.grin.com is an ideal platform for presenting term papers, final papers, scientific essays, dissertations and specialist books.

Visit us on the internet:

http://www.grin.com/

http://www.facebook.com/grincom

http://www.twitter.com/grin_com

Women & ICT

3/29/2014

Paul Onwurah , Hyellamanda Musa, Tombari Biranen, Chidinma Orji,
Donmike Uwagwu & Abdul-Samad Mohammed

Introduction

The world is changing and will still change more, only at an ever-increasing pace. The events and innovations of the last few centuries have served as testaments to the validity of this fact. The influence that science, technology and more recently, ICT have had on the world's dynamics cannot be overrated or over emphasized. ICT for example has become one of the strongest forces of the modern world, with applications in virtually every facet of human existence, from medicine to communications; transportation to entertainment; defense to artificial intelligence.

Unfortunately, statistics have shown that women's participation in IT and technology in general is low and declining. Berryman (1983) used the 'leaky pipeline' metaphor to describe the attrition of women from science and technology in general. The leaky pipeline is used to describe the "continuous loss of women in science and technology as they climb the career ladder" (Muffit, 2014). It has also been noted that employment opportunities for women in technological and engineering fields have been very low especially in areas such as the computer industry (Hoffmann-Barthes, Nair, & Malpede).

This paper seeks primarily to evaluate the low participation of women in technology and ICT, and to identify the obstacles hindering higher participation, in a bid to proffering solutions that will eliminate or at least reduce the effect of the obstacles.

Women's Participation in IT: a Global Perspective

The absence of women in computing has been largely noticed around the world. It has also been noticed that the entry of women into IT education and employment is not only low, but also steadily declining in most countries (Castano & Webster, 2012). The maximum share of females in IT-related degree courses in OECD countries about 30%, and as low as under 10% in some countries. Low participation rates have also been noticed in a large number of developed countries. In the US for example, it is estimated that only 25% of IT specialists are women, with figures as low as 20% in Northern Europe. It has also been noted that between the year 2000 and 2013 [a period when the number of young women in virtually every field including sciences has increased], there hasn't been any significant increase in the percentage of women in ICT. These trends have raised concerns and many have sought to identify the factors preventing an equal increase of women in ICT education and careers.

1

Reasons for low participation of women in ICT and Technology

A review of several scholarly works has shown that the reasons for women's low participation in ICT and Technology are countless and vary as each society has its own peculiarities. Generally, however, the factors that affect women's low participation can be classified in three groups; barriers related to acquisition of technological education, barriers related to employment of females for tech related roles, and barriers related to culture and tradition. Cultural barriers have however been noticed to be the meeting point between educational and employment-related factors causing low participation of women in ICT and technological careers.

Education-based Barriers to Participation

Education in general, like most social systems is strongly influenced by gender disparities. School boys and girls are made to see some subjects as more appropriate/useful to girls and other subjects are made to seem more appropriate for males. As a result, "girls rarely receive positive encouragement to try the technical and scientific subjects for which boys are supposed to have a natural aptitude" (Hoffmann-Barthes, Nair, & Malpede).

Several theories have been advanced in an attempt to identify the reasons for the low percentage of women who enroll into science and technology courses. Scholars such as King and Hill (1993) have stated that the factors specific factors hindering women's enrollment into technological education and IT may vary from setting to setting, and the major challenge is to identify the prime factors hindering women's' ICT participation in individual socio-cultural settings (Evans, 1995).

Evans (1995) identified five kinds of barriers that are most likely to prevent women from participation in ICT. They include:

- Cultural Barriers
- Attitudinal Barriers
- Qualificatory Barriers
- Situational Barriers and
- Institutional Barriers

Cultural Barriers: Culture has been identified to be one of the greatest barriers of women's participation in ICT and technology at large. Studies have proven that common patterns exist in the role and perception of the status of women across societies, regardless of the different circumstances and peculiarities. In most societies, cultural and traditional norms have forced the woman to be perceived as subservient being (Evans, 1995). This status has unfortunately forced females around the world conform to traditional female career choices. Culture causes most females to make career choices based on gender stereotypes, and because ICT careers carry a "gender label", very few women take ICT and technology seriously as a career option. (Castano & Webster, 2012)

Attitudinal Barriers: According to Evans, this kind of barrier emanate from the perceived differences in the capabilities of males and females. Castano and Webster (2012) stated that these perceived differences in the capabilities of males and females begin in the family where "gender stereotypes are constructed and enacted". The gender divide is further broadened by schooling, peer pressure, and the scarcity of female role models and results in lack of confidence and low self-esteem.

Qualificatory: This kind of barrier as identified by Evans comes into being as a result of the absence of prerequisites such as Math and science courses. Evan however suggests evidence proves that this barrier is perceived rather than real. Ellis (1987) found that in many countries, women with general requirements to study sciences end up studying human and social science courses in the university.

Situational Barriers: These barriers are faced in attending courses or practicing ICT, they consist of several factors such as family commitments, lack of support from spouses and family. Evans also stated that women also face a financial barrier in terms of fees and cost of study materials as they do not have independent control of family finances/resources thus they have to rely on the support of their male partners who ate mostly unsupportive in most cases. Male partners are less likely to support their spouses' entry into study courses and careers that are traditionally perceived as "male-oriented".

Some scholars such have however noticed that gender interact with social class factors in significant ways. King and Hill for example noticed that women with some of these situational

3

barriers such as domestic labor and lack of finance have less influence on women who posses higher social class status. They noticed that in many developed and developing nations, upper class women pursue their educational and career aspirations by paying women to take care domestic labor and other factors that would have otherwise constitute barriers.

Institutional Barriers: This class of barriers, Evans identified, arise because of the manner in which institutions make their programs available. They are barriers that arise due to the inflexibility of technological programs as offered in conventional colleges and universities. These general institutional barriers affecting women's education [not only in ICT and tech] include lack of flexibility of lecture hours, substantial lecture attendance requirement, and lack of child care facilities etc. Evans however stated that the aforementioned barriers are exacerbated in the case of technical and technological studies by the absence of female instructors and negative attitude of male teachers; male orientation in courses' publicity etc.

Employment-related Barriers

Several employment-related barrier to the participation of women in ICT and technology have been identified, one of which is the gender pay gap – the difference between the wages paid to men and women, often for doing the same work (Castano & Webster, 2012). Gender pay gap has been shown to affect women's participation in ICT negatively. In the European Union for example, where the gender pay gap of IT professionals has increased drastically overt time, the proportion of women in IT-related jobs has remain stagnant at 0.7%.The fact that women are largely expected by culture/tradition to end up as child bearers and housewives has also negatively influenced the participation of women in technology in particular and any form of employment in general, especially in the developing regions of the world such as Sub-Saharan Africa (Victor, Payton, Kvasny, & Amadi, 2007)

The Way Forward

Gender Equality

It will be impossible to improve women's participation in ICT without addressing all of the gender-related factors militating against improved participation of women in ICT. Issues such as the gender pay gap must be addressed and all bias in the enrollment of females into to ICT and tech-related education must be eliminated.

Policy Making

Cases in US and Canada have proved that policy making can be very useful in increasing women's participation in ICT and technological education in general. It is important to set up policies and agencies to specially cater for the recruitment of females into the field of ICT and technology. In the University of Alberta, Canada, a taskforce, Women in Scholarship, Engineering, Science and Technology (WISEST) was set up in a bid to increasing the participation of women in Science, Technology and Engineering. WISEST is recorded to have achieved its goals and objectives to a large extent by fostering support among women and staff of higher learning institutions. (Badekale, 2003)

Long Distance Education and ICT's role

Evans (1995) suggested the use of long distance education to improve women's participation in technological and ICT careers. Long distance education can help improve participation of women in ICT in many ways. IT-powered long distance programs can help to reduce the extent to which barriers such as family commitment and domestic labor affect women's enrollment into technological education by creating platforms for extreme flexibility. Evans highlighted three forms of programs which could be used to increase the enrollment of women into ICT based courses: bridging programs, conversion programs and community-based programs. Bridging programs via distance education, Evans noticed, could assist greatly in updating and reentry for women who had already possessed the requirements for technological and ICT courses. Evans also observed that conversion programs could aid first entry into technological education for older women and early school leavers who wish to change direction from mainstream female courses.

Conclusion

The low participation of women in ICT and technology is obviously depriving the field of a vast amount of human resources and talents. The information in this paper has identified that there several barriers preventing an increase in the percentage of women involved in ICT careers and tech. These barriers have however been noticed to affect participation in varying degree depending on the society in question. It is therefore necessary to identify which barriers affect which communities the most, and to ensure that adequate measures are taken to eliminate or at least substantially reduce the influence of the barriers. Barriers such as gender pay gap and gender inequality must however be addressed globally if any improvement is to be made.

References

Badekale, A. J. (2003). Women and Engineering in Nigeria: Towards Improved Policy Initiatives and Increased Female Participation. *ATPS Working Paper Series No. 37* , 1-63.

Castano, C., & Webster, J. (2012). Understanding Women's Presence in ICT: the Life Course Perspective. *International Journal of Gender, Science and Technology* , 365-386.

Ellis, P. (1990). *Measures Increasing the Participation of Girls and Women in Technical and Vocational Education: A Caribbean Study.* London: CommonWealth.

European Commission Information Society. (2010). *Women and ICT Status Report 2009.* European Commission Information Society.

Evans, K. (1995). *Barriers to Participation of Women in Technological Education and the Role of Distance Education.* The Commonwealth of Learning.

Hafkin, N., & Huyer, S. (2007). Women and Gender in ICT: Statistics and Indicators for Development. *Information Technologies and International Development , 4* (2), 25-41.

Hoffmann-Barthes, A. M., Nair, S., & Malpede, D. *Scientific , Technical and Vocational Education of Girls in Africa.* Sumary of 21 Reports.

King, E., & Hill, M. (1993). *Women's Education in Developing Countries: Barriers, Benefits and Policies.* Baltimore: John Hopkins University Press.

Muffit, E. (2014, February 14). *The 'leaky pipeline' of women in science.* Retrieved March 26, 2014, from Telegraph: http://www.telegraph.co.uk/education/educationopinion/10637941/the-leaky-pipeline-of-women-in-science.html

Taeb, M., Irmtraud, M., Govind, K., Peilei, F., Marilia, G. d., & Nageen, A. (2005). *Revisiting Women's Participation in Science and Technology: Emerging Challenges and Agenda for Reform.* United Nations University Institute of Advanced Studies.

Victor, M., Payton, F. C., Kvasny, L., & Amadi, A. (2007). IT Education and Workforce Participation A New Era for Women in Kenya. *The Information Society* , 1-19.